Running
the Race with the
ONE

I Love You,
I'm With You & All Is Well!

Lou Richardson

WESTBOW
P R E S S®
A DIVISION OF THOMAS NELSON
& ZONDERVAN

Scripture taken from the King James Version of the Bible.

This book is a work of non-fiction. Unless otherwise noted, the author and the publisher make no explicit guarantees as to the accuracy of the information contained in this book and in some cases, names of people and places have been altered to protect their privacy.

WestBow Press books may be ordered through booksellers or by contacting:

WestBow Press
A Division of Thomas Nelson & Zondervan
1663 Liberty Drive
Bloomington, IN 47403
www.westbowpress.com
1 (866) 928-1240

Author Photo by Maurice Wells
inhisimagew@att.net

ISBN: 978-1-5127-8107-6 (sc)
ISBN: 978-1-5127-8108-3 (hc)
ISBN: 978-1-5127-8106-9 (e)

Library of Congress Control Number: 2017904481

Print information available on the last page.

WestBow Press rev. date: 04/07/2017

To my Lord and Savior, I give all glory.

I love You, Lord. You are amazing. If it had not been for the Lord, I would not be here today, writing His book.

When I began to write this book, I did not yet have the title for it; I called it *His Book*.

The words I knew had to come from Him; I did not know how to begin or how to put my experiences into words.

I wanted to tell the world, but did not know how to begin. I had so many thoughts racing through my mind, but I did not know where to begin to speak to my readers.

But He placed a powerful woman in my path: His servant, an author, and a coach.

She gave me a direction to take that blessed me, and so I began to write.

I remember her first words to me were "Sit down in a quiet place and begin to write." She told me to write as if I were having a conversation with one person because my thoughts were, *How am I going to tell everybody my story? There's so much I want to say to help others who may be going through this or to help a loved one or friend; what do I say?*

Her words to me were, "No, don't think of it that way; just write as if you are having a conversation with one person, someone who's asking you questions about cancer and your experiences. Answer that person."

I found this to be so helpful, and it made my writing so much easier.

Blessings, Coach. I am thankful that our paths crossed. Won't He do it!

Running the Race with the One is also dedicated to all cancer survivors and overcomers.

You may be picking up this book facing a cancer diagnosis; this is why I was urged to write this book, in the hope that these penned words will help you fight for life, not only this life but eternal life. Never give up on our Lord, the healer, and never give up the fight. You may give out, but don't give up.

Remember, this too shall pass.

As an encouragement, no matter how tedious the journey or difficult the fight, keep fighting.

And in memory of those diagnosed, who fought courageously and lost the battle to this dreadful disease: You are not forgotten; your memory is alive.

I honor you with the writing of this book.

"I have fought a good fight, I have finished my course, I have kept the faith: Henceforth there is laid up for me a crown of righteousness, which the Lord, the Righteous Judge, shall give me at that day: and not to me only, but unto all them also that love his appearing" (2 Timothy 4:7–8 KJV).

As you are with Jesus, you know that it was all worth it.

Contents

Introduction
Lou's Take

My first thoughts about the diagnosis was, *Is this real?*

What? Not me! This can't be happening.

I must be having a nightmare; I will awaken to find that it was all just a bad dream.

I've heard about others who have been diagnosed, but not me.

Why do we always think, *Not me?*

I've heard stories about cancer, even as early as an adolescent, when our neighbor was diagnosed with breast cancer, but I never thought it would be me.

I look back and recall the day I heard the word "cancer" and the word "malignant" from my radiologist, after having my left breast biopsied.

I recall the look on the nurse's face when she said, "I'll be right back," to the radiologist; that look confirmed what I'd already suspected.

After the ultrasound, the radiologist said, "Ms. Richardson, we want to schedule a biopsy."

She wanted to prove what she already knew.

I must say that after hearing all of that, I did not hear much else. My memory is foggy from that moment.

And everything spoken after the "c" word seemed to be a fading bunch of sounds.

After the biopsy confirmed the mass was malignant, I was told that I had breast cancer and would need to move forward ASAP.

I would need to schedule an appointment with an oncologist and a surgeon.

I was provided with a few names of oncologists and surgeons.

The oncologist and surgeon would determine whether they'd perform a mastectomy or lumpectomy of my left breast.

I do recall the nurse asking if I had a doctor in mind; no, as I've never been diagnosed with cancer.

And no one in my family had ever had cancer.

Many thoughts entered my mind on the drive home. It was the longest drive ever. And to this day, I don't remember being behind the wheel.

After arriving home, I decided to call a meeting with my children and tell them.

I wondered what their reaction to this unexpected and shocking news would be.

I thought of my dad of eighty-plus years and about my siblings and friends. My thoughts were going a hundred miles per second.

So many things that we take for granted and choose not to let enter our thoughts.

When we are told such unexpected, shocking health news, so many ideas start developing.

In my prayers, I asked the Lord, was it something I did? Was I not exercising enough, eating properly ... what?

What do I do now?

I guess these reactions are normal.

I began looking back over my life: how was I eating, exercising (or not), what type of foods could have contributed to this disease? Had I been eating too much of this or not enough of that? What about the amount of coffee I'd consumed, or maybe not enough water? Should I have taken more vitamins?

But then, why did it have to be anything that I did (or did not do)?

Maybe this was my storm that I had to go through, my test to take.

It felt like I had been shaken and spoken to, saying, "Trust Me, daughter.

Will you trust Me?" He asked. "Do you believe that I can do all things but fail; do you believe my Word as you profess to believe? Trust Me."

My heavenly Father said, "I have the final word. I know the plan that I have for you."

When you recall the scripture, this is when you are so grateful that you are rooted and grounded in His Word.

You are thankful that you have the Word of the Lord on

the tablet of your heart, that you can now pull it up, speak it out, and apply the Word to your life now.

It's the Word that heals you spiritually, that develops you and prepares you to persevere physically in the natural world, to press on even as the fiery darts come your way; you are shielded and protected.

You just have to go through and stand on the Word. He promises to always be with you.

It's the Word that saves; it is the Word that delivers and set free those who are captive, those who feel like life is over. It's not over until He says it's over.

It's the Word that gives you hope; that *is* your hope.

Believe the Word; it speaks life into your situation and can make death behave.

Our heavenly Father is greater than any disease known to man. Greater is He that is in me than he that is in the world.

Father, I thank you today that as I pass the baton, just as track and field runners do on a relay team. Keep moving the baton until it reaches the last person (symbolically, the baton represents the Word).

I pass it on. I trust You, Lord. And I will never doubt You.

My message to all who have been diagnosed with cancer or faced some other obstacle. Whatever your test may be on this journey, allow it to be your testimony; most importantly, through it all, trust Him.

The Word heals, sets free, destroys yokes. So trust, believe, and live the Word.

"In the beginning, was the Word and the Word was with God, and the Word was God" (John 1:1 KJV).

I continue to pass it on, and the Word goes on and on, until it has reached all whom God has intended; He desires that none perish.

Pass on His Word until the end of the earth.

As believers, we are His messengers and witnesses; we are fulfillers of His purpose for our lives.

He knows the plan that He has for us, plans for good and not evil, for hope and future, to prosper us.

I believe; therefore, I shall live and not die, that I may declare His Word, to decree and declare to His goodness.

Never give up on Jesus, no matter what it looks like, no matter what it smells like; always trust and never doubt.

"Ask, and it shall be given you; seek, and ye shall find; knock, and it shall be opened unto you" (Matthew 7:7 KJV).

And we will all meet up together at the beginning, never ending. A new beginning, eternally.

The race leads us to Jesus. He's the winner. We are His vessels.

Running the Race with the One

Foreword

Lou Richardson has written an unselfish testimony of her own personal journey of how Jesus Christ healed her from the devastation of cancer; she lovingly shares her humanity and discloses the principles she used in facing and defeating the giants in her life.

If you only read one book this year, you have it in your hands. This fine piece of writing will impact your life forever.

As a pastor and bishop and on behalf of the City Cathedral Church, One Church in Three Locations in Houston, I am proud to have the opportunity to express my sentiment on this wonderful work.

Bishop Leroy J. Woodard, Jr.

Acknowledgments

To my sweet mother, a precious woman, Willie Mae Richardson: You taught me so much about love, and I saw your love for our heavenly Father and for the family. You are resting in His arms. He picked a beautiful flower for His garden, and you left a sweet aroma with your human family that will last forever. I love you, Medea, always and forever.

Thank you for your sweet, unconditional love.

I remember as a child I did not always behave, but you always loved me; you hugged me and kissed me and forgave me in spite of my actions. I miss you.

Medea, you taught me to always be a lady; you prayed for me and taught me the Lord's Prayer as a child growing up.

You taught me the Word by precept and example in the way you lived your life before me. You showed me how to love and take care of a husband and family without saying a word, sometimes just by doing and being yourself. I love you.

To my daddy, Roosevelt Richardson, a great man and a mighty prayer warrior. Daddy, you are a man with wisdom and knowledge. You move mountains with your prayers.

Your faith is strong in the Lord. You taught me, by

example, what I should observe in a man; you treated our mother like the queen she was. And for that, I love and respect you so much.

You taught me to keep God as the center of my life and to always wait for His direction. Thank you, Daddy, for teaching me to give and that it will be given unto me, good measure, pressed down, shaken together, and running over will men pour into my lap.

Thank you, Daddy. I love you.

To my sister, Gloria: How can I just say thank you?

You have a humble spirit and a loving heart, and you are such a giver.

Thank you, sister, for all that you do. I love you with all my heart.

I know that I have expressed how much you are appreciated and loved in words and deeds, but here it is again: I love you, sister.

I cherish our sister bond, our friendship that has grown over the years, and it continues to grow even more.

I am thankful to the Lord for you, my sister, and for your endless love. You give of yourself and your time, and you have a special gift of finding a unique gift for those special occasions.

I am always excited when you say to me, "I have something for you."

You have a huge heart, one of gold, and you are the best, the greatest sister anyone could ever imagine.

I am thankful that the Lord blessed me to have you as my sister.

Thank you for coming to my bedside after surgery and massaging my back and praying for me (I heard and felt your prayers).

I love you, sister. Glory to His name.

To my big brother, Willie (Chunk): I love you so much. And thank you for the prayers. I know you prayed for me. I felt them. I know you love me, although you are a man of few words.

But your actions speak louder than words could ever say.

I love you, and I appreciate you so much. I enjoy the many lunches and dinners we've shared together; we spent time just sitting, laughing, and talking.

Those times meant the most to me. Thank you, big brother, for your spirit of giving; the things you do may seem small to you, but they speak volumes to me.

I realize that Medea and Daddy taught each of us how to give, but I am so thankful that we grabbed hold of this and passed it on to our children.

I am proud that you are my brother. I love you.

To my brother, B.C. (my twin, as I like to call him): I love you.

When we were younger, people used to say that we resembled each other so much; I always smiled.

I remember my first visit to California; you and Sandy took me around to meet your friends, and I was so proud and felt so special. You always showed your love for me in words and actions; I am proud to be your little sister. You always make me laugh, making up funny songs about my nickname and telling me funny jokes.

As I write this, I am smiling in remembrance of those times. Even though you are thousands of miles away, know that you are always near to me in my heart.

I always pray for you, brother, and I love you.

To Dean, Sandy, and David: Even though you are married to my siblings, you are my sisters, Dean and Sandy, and you are my brother, David. I have never thought of you as in-laws, only as sisters and my brother.

I love each of you so much, and you have made my siblings jubilant in their marriage to each of you, and for that I am grateful. And I love each of you.

Dean: Wow, sis. We have much history between us: more than fifty years. I love you, Deannie Gal. You have a unique place in my heart as a tear-jerker.

You were born to be a Richardson, and I can't remember you ever being anyone else. You are a born giver.

I always smile at the memories of you. We always went out to eat; whether it was rainy or sunny, we were out together at a seven-star restaurant.

I also remember our days when we worked together; you taught me so much, and I am grateful, my sister.

You are a giver of your time, your love, and your finances.

Thank you for always being yourself: a great wife to my brother, and a great mother to my niece and nephews.

I love you, sister.

Sandy, my sister, I love you. Thank you for always opening your heart and your home to me whenever I came to visit you guys in California.

From the very first time we met, we bonded with laughter, and you would always call me Skinny Tail Gal.

We hit it off right away, and I remember how you would dance; you and my brother would two-step, and wow: You really could get down with him. LOL.

I love you, Sandy, and I thank you for loving my brother and for being a great wife, a dear sister to me, and a great mother to my nieces and nephews. I love you.

David, my brother, I love you. Thank you for your prayers and for always treating me like your sister.

You have always treated me with great respect and love.

Thank you for always opening your home to me and for cooking those great meals at Thanksgiving and Christmas; even when you weren't feeling your best, you sacrificed so that we would have a nice spread, and it was always delicious. Thanks, brother.

Thank you for always thinking of me on my birthday and at Christmas.

Every year, I always looked forward to your unique gifts; they are always different and very special, and you always seem to give me exactly what I needed for my home.

Thank you for loving Gloria, my sister, and taking care of her and my nieces and nephew. Be blessed. I love you.

To my children: Tamika, Delinda, Maurice, and Ali:

From the time I called the family meeting to announce the doctors' result from the biopsy, you all were very supportive.

Each of you agreed that you would be with me and stand by me through it all, and you were so supportive (you still are). I love you all so much. Thank you for your prayers, love, and patience with me, the patient.

Thank you for giving your time to transport me to and from the many doctor visits and treatments, also for visiting me, bringing me food, and being caregivers.

To my grandchildren: I love each one of you. I cherish you and am so grateful for being able to watch you grow into outstanding young men and women. I could not be more proud of each of you. Be blessed and keep the Word first in your lives.

To my extended family: thank you to those who bless me and honor me with words of affection and endearment by calling me Mom; thanks also to my friends who cooked for me, prayed with me, and supported in so many ways.

To my wonderful spiritual father, Bishop Leroy J. Woodard Jr., who is a great leader and who prays for me and has supported me in writing this book: I love you past the moon! Be blessed.

To my City Cathedral Church family: Thank you all for your support of me and this book and for your encouraging words that kept reminding me that "I can do it" with divine inspiration. Thank you for your prayers; it is now published, and you're reading His book: *Running the Race with the One.*

I love you all. Be blessed.

Letters from Loved Ones

To My Only Sister

When I first learned of my sister Lou's diagnosis with cancer, I was so sad and so depressed.

I went in prayer and asked Him, "Why is this happening to my only sister? She has been through so much: a marriage that didn't work out and other trials."

Now this, the most devastating thing that I could ever think of: cancer.

Thank You, Lord, my heavenly Father that my sister has been so faithful, and that she has always been such a help to me and my small problems. Lord, she is a blessing to many.

Now she is facing the biggest test of all, cancer, but it will be to show the family that through this journey, you must have faith. You have nothing if you don't have faith.

I love you, my sister.
—Gloria Burks

The Day I Remember

I remember the day I received the message
that my sister was very ill; I remember
falling to my knees, sad and worried.
I was hoping she would get through this
and be all right. I prayed, asking the Lord to
let her live and not let my sister die.
But then after talking with my other sister,
Gloria, I felt a lot better. I said to myself, *She is
strong, she loves the Lord, and she will be okay.*
I know my sister Lou is unyielding, and I prayed. My
thoughts were with you every day until I talked to
you after the surgery; I knew you would be okay.
I remember you telling me that everything was in our
heavenly Father's hand, so I didn't worry any more.
The Lord will take care of you; this was
the day I will always remember.

Your brother,
Bobby Charles (B.C.)

I Just Want to Say

I want to say, I love you very much.

I am thankful for you and for being a part of my life.

If I go home tomorrow to be with the Lord, you just stay like you are because you are a child of the King. Keep on praying and remain faithful.

I wish I were able to do more for you. I love you; you are like my daughter.

We have so much fun together, and I enjoy being with you.

I am so thankful for you. I can talk to you because you understand me.

All I am saying is, I love you.

Be blessed, baby.

Mama
Ann Brooks

To God be All Glory

Wow, Mom, you asked me to give my testimony about this ugly disease called cancer. I know this was a test of our family's love, patience, endurance, and strength. This whirlwind experience took me through many emotions in just a short time, but it was the right time, as He saw fit.

At that point, I had rededicated my life to my Savior. Satan was very disturbed by that and went after my only child, trying to disrupt our lives. But as a family, we stood on our heavenly Father's promises for my daughter's life and your life, and we continue to give Him all the glory. The enemy raised his head and tried to attack you with cancer. You had confessed your calling to proclaim the gospel, and Satan wanted to defeat this journey, but he was blocked.

Mom, you called a family meeting to inform us of what would take place with the doctors, hospital stay, chemotherapy, and radiation. At that point, I was in shock, trying to understand what was going to happen with our family. After the meeting, I went home and started praying, asking for preparation mentally, physically, and spiritually for this trial and journey. As we entered this whirlwind as a family, we prayed and talked to friends, asking them to pray and sending prayer requests to all believers.

During this time of preparation, the Lord gave you peace about the situation; you said that He told you, "All is well, and I'm with you."

You received test results from the doctors that confirmed that you had this ugly disease, cancer. But you said that you had put on the whole armor and would win this war.

The day of your surgery, we prayed with family and friends and waited for the miracle He was completing in the operating room; we knew that all was well.

After surgery, the doctor came to the waiting room to give us the report of the Lord; we all knew that it was His report, and that's the report we would believe.

The doctor told us that he removed all the cancer he saw and that you should recover well.

After the procedure, the hospital staff rolled you to your room; we all waited for your arrival. You looked very peaceful, like the diva you are.

My mom is a diva. You would have to know her, and then you would understand that she takes care to look beautiful from head to toe.

After arriving at your room, you stretched out your arms, as if you knew we were all there, but being so sedated, I can't imagine that you were coherent enough to know anything at that point. But amazingly, you went into prayer.

Mom, you wanted nothing more than to give all the glory to our heavenly Father for what He had done for you and our family. Thank You, Lord.

For a couple of days, Delinda and I rotated nights, staying at the hospital with you. During my stay with you, I would watch you sleep and pray for a healing of your body. I asked Him to allow you to continue your journey of proclaiming

His Word, to create in you a new spirit. I prayed that you would be totally free from cancer.

This experience allowed me to draw closer to my Lord and to know that we will continue to stand on His Word as a family. We will not look back but look forward, knowing that the Lord can do all things.

Thank You, Lord, for Your healing in my mother's body, mind, and soul, to still be able to proclaim Your Word and bring lost souls to You, Lord.

Glory.
Tamika Perry

To HIM all Glory and Praises

Momma, this was an experience that I wish you didn't have to endure, but I thank the Lord it came out the way that it did. As I write this, I cry because I know what He has done (and is still doing). The impact was spiritual for me as well as emotional, but we all know that I am emotional. When we had our initial meeting at your house, it was just a test, but the second meeting, when you said that the doctor diagnosed cancer, terrified me. But time went on, and after your surgery, we were in recovery mode, to make sure all was done to make you comfortable and get you well as fast as possible.

The hospital was stressful for me, but I couldn't show it. I spoke to my friend; we had prayed before I arrived at your house. I spoke to him about my fears, but my friend was my rock when I needed to cry or scream or ask what was next. He was very supportive and stayed with me at the hospital during most of the night. There were so many people who were praying for you and who showed up at the hospital; it was a relief to have others there with you.

Your pastor and his wife stayed the entire time while you were in surgery, and others came later, and there were so many calls. Daddy called a lot too. The operation continued on past the two and a half hours it was supposed to take; we all became worried. Finally, the doctor came out and gave us the news that all was well. We were just happy that it went well and that it was over.

The family walked alongside as they rolled you to your room, and as usual, you looked like a sleeping diva.

It was a blessing when you awoke and began to pray; that was when I knew everything was going to be okay. That was the sign I needed, when you awakened and went into prayer. I spent many days at your house, which was good, but sometimes, when I couldn't be in two places at once, my house and yours, it was stressful. But the Lord worked it out that my children's father took them when I needed to be with you. He worked it all out to where you recovered enough to take more care of yourself without our being there all the time. The Lord even sent others to take care of you when I had to return to work and was not able to be there with you.

Peace is what we received. Praise You, Lord.
Your daughter,
Delinda

Survivor Stories

Cecilia (CeCe) Herd

My story begins in October 2008, when I did a self-exam and found a small lump on my right breast. I went to my primary doctor, and she felt it also. She scheduled me for a diagnostic mammogram. The mammogram detected a second lump that we were not able to feel. I went on to have a biopsy to see if they were malignant or benign. While I waited for the results, I consulted the Lord in intensity about this. He said, "Do not be afraid, I have you." The test results came back, and the results were the dreaded C-word. I decided not to tell anyone but my husband. At that time, he was living in another state and was about to rejoin us, so I pressed the urgency to speed up his move. Once he arrived, we made an appointment with the surgeon my primary care doctor recommended. We met with this doctor but were not pleased with his insensitivity. He said I should go ahead and have a mastectomy because there were two lumps. We were not satisfied with his answer and sought another opinion. We found a more skilled surgeon who said that she could remove both lumps, without having to do a mastectomy.

At this time, I finally told the rest of my family. They all scolded me for going through the diagnostic and the biopsy without telling them. I apologized but let them know I could not let any doubt or unbelief get in. I proceeded to have the surgery. After many weeks of recovery, my husband decided that he no longer wanted to live with me. He wanted to return to his previous home. This left me devastated. Cancer, now divorce. I had to go through chemotherapy and radiation alone.

My daughter, LaTonya, stepped up to the plate to be my caregiver. I went through these treatments from April to July 2009, then I was able to return to work in August. It was a strenuous task to return to work, but my sick leave was depleted; therefore, I had no choice. Before I went through my chemotherapy and radiation treatments, I was introduced to Lou Richardson, the author of this book, through a mutual friend. Little did I know she would be my saving grace. She went through her treatments first; therefore, she could share with me what to do and what to expect. I praise my heavenly Father for our divine friendship during this time in both of our lives. Now it has been eight years down the road, and we are still the best of friends. Our journey wasn't easy, but with the help of each other and the help of the Lord, we don't look like what we've been though.

—Cecilia (CeCe) Herd

Gayle Woodard

In the summer of 2015, I was diagnosed with stage one B-cell skin lymphoma.

After noticing symptoms that appeared to be alopecia on my scalp, I saw a dermatologist, who gave me a biopsy and diagnosed me with lymphoma cancer.

It is important to be proactive in managing your health. When cancer is involved, time is of the essence. My antibiotic treatment (Rituximab Infusion RTN) worked because of early detection. This can eliminate the need for chemotherapy and radiation. If you suspect that something may be wrong with your body, see a doctor as soon as possible. If you detect something wrong with your scalp, covering it with extensions, wigs, or over-the-counter creams will not prepare you for healing. Having faith and knowledge will prepare you for healing. If this circumstance is familiar to you, seek understanding and confidence through prayer. I thank my heavenly Father that I am a survivor.

Be blessed,
Gayle Woodard

Therese Moira Flaherty

Thank you, dear Lou (my friend, co-survivor, coworker), for honoring me by allowing me to share my personal journey of surviving breast cancer. And thank you, Lord, for sparing my life twice within one year.

The year 2009 was a difficult one for me. In the spring, I was recovering from a car accident that left me with a very sore body. While having my annual wellness exam, my gynecologist discovered a new lump and convinced me that I had put off having my annual mammogram for too long. That was the first year I'd ever skipped my regularly scheduled mammogram. What a terrible decision that turned out to be.

With my sore body, I wasn't looking forward to a breast-crushing mammogram, but I knew it had to be done. The screening mammogram found suspicious tissue in my left breast. I have dense breast tissue, and this had been the result of many previous mammograms. I wasn't concerned when the doctor prescribed a diagnostic mammogram and ultrasound procedure.

Two weeks later, I was relieved that the breast center allowed me to skip the diagnostic mammogram and go straight to the ultrasound procedure because the first mammogram was so painful. The ultrasound revealed a cyst behind the suspicious mass of tissue. Now, I was concerned but not scared.

I wasn't frightened until I received a phone call saying

that a biopsy was required. I'd been through this series of tests before but never made it all the way to the biopsy stage. Cancer had always been ruled out before I'd gotten to that level of testing.

Early on the morning of July 6, the doctor aspirated the cyst and performed a needle biopsy on the suspicious mass. Then more bad news: A second mass was found, and another biopsy was needed. Now, I was really scared. I left that appointment in tears.

Three days later, I received the dreaded news: I had breast cancer. I was overwhelmed with feelings of devastation and sadness but still wondering if my doctor called the right person. Less than two weeks later, I received the same diagnosis on the second biopsy.

I immediately made an appointment with a breast surgeon.

They say that when you are diagnosed with a serious illness, you go through the five stages of grief. By the time I saw my doctor, I was full-on into the second stage, which is anger. I was mad and blamed the breast center for not having found the cancerous tumors earlier. Then, I was devastated to learn that I'd be losing my natural nipples during the mastectomy surgery. My doctor was extremely compassionate and eased my fears.

Even though I had cancer in only one breast, I opted for a double mastectomy because breast cancer was prevalent in both sides of my family. I certainly didn't want to ever have to experience it again. During my surgery, lymph nodes were removed to determine if the tumor was invasive. Out of sixteen lymph nodes, five were found positive for cancer. With the skilled hands of my doctor and tons of prayers from family and friends, I've been cancer-free since September 8, 2009, the date of my surgery.

Immediately following the mastectomy, my plastic surgeon started the process of breast reconstruction, using tissue expanders. The expanders promoted skin growth, and I received saline injections to restore my bust to its previous size.

During breast reconstruction mode, while I received chemotherapy treatments, my loving sister and my mother were at my side (just talking, reading, or playing card games). I always heard that patients could become violently ill while receiving chemotherapy, and I was fearful that it would happen to me; however, through the power of prayer and antinausea medication, I was never very sick. The first session had me bedridden for a couple of days, but after the last session, I had no side effects at all.

Once I completed four cycles of chemotherapy, I was scheduled for thirty radiation treatments. I really didn't want to have radiation five days a week for six weeks, until I found out that if I didn't, there was a 40 percent chance the cancer would return. That percentage was just too high for me; I had to do it. As it turned out, it was painless and more of a nuisance than anything else. I followed my radiation oncologist's advice and had no skin problems from the treatment, only swelling of the area.

With sixteen lymph nodes removed, my lymphatic system had been compromised; ironically, radiation actually promotes lymphedema, so while I was receiving radiation treatment, I sought out lymphedema prevention treatment, as well. It was then that I met the owner of HOPE Lymphedema Treatment Center, who eventually became my friend and helped heal me physically and emotionally.

After the swelling receded, I had surgery to replace the uncomfortable tissue expanders with softer, silicone breast implants. Later, after nipple reconstruction surgery and tattooing of the areolae, I finally felt and looked natural again. I didn't care that they were artificial; thanks be to our heavenly Father, I was still alive.

Somewhere along my journey, my medical leave of absence expired, and I lost my job. If it hadn't been for my giving parents, I don't know where I'd be. I look back and realize this was a blessing in disguise, as I was able to continue my health insurance and receive treatment without being stressed out about missing time at the office.

Although I had minimal issues after multiple surgeries, all is not perfect: over time, my man-made nipples were absorbed by my body, and due to the radiation treatments, the fat graft procedure (moving fat from my tummy to fill in around the upper breast area) caused fat necrosis (my affected breast was hardened). My plastic surgeon had warned me about these possible results. I will have the harden fat removed one day, but for now (praise the Lord!), there's a lot more of life to be living, and I'm proud to exclaim, "I am a breast cancer survivor."

—Therese Moira Flaherty

Chapter 1

Real-Life Story

First, let me start by saying that this isn't what I would have chosen as any part of my life story, but the Lord has brought me through it. I'm His vessel, used for His glory. What the enemy meant for evil, the Lord has turned around for my good. No weapon formed against me shall prosper.

Designed to help others, I call this His book because it is. This book is His story about my journey. The script was provided to me. I am His vessel. Use me, Lord, for your glory.

The Lord is my director, and I'm the actor in this story. He knows the plan He has for me.

As I sit and write about what I've endured, I wondered why I was placed in this situation. I know now it was a test that I may learn and grow spiritually. Run the race with endurance. Press in, press my way through. I'm not alone. I run with the One, my creator.

I'm running this race with the One to reach the finals. I'm running with endurance to reach the goal, the prize of a higher calling on my life.

I thought as a writer that I would be able to write non-stop because of all the information that was stored in my heart, the seed of my mind, but sometimes it seemed there's only one paragraph per sitting.

Lord, I believe that I have writer's block. What's up? But He is aware of my thoughts before I think them, and He knows the end from the beginning. He's alpha and omega. And His book would be completed in His timing.

The enemy may try to defeat, distract, and oppress on every hand, but he has no place in us. We're children of the most high God.

As you go through tough times, stay rooted and grounded in the Word. You can do all things through Christ who strengthens you. And I know that as believers, we already have the victory. He has overcome the world, and therefore we're also overcomers. We're more than conquerors. He's our provider, and our protector. I love when He protects me, thank you Lord!

I have written this book and it is my journey on what I had to go through. You may ask why would anyone have to go through so much? Well, you can also ask yourself why not? Remember what His Word says: We're His heirs, and sometimes we must suffer through things, but we'll also reign as He reigns.

He's my creator, and He knows me better than anyone (even better than I know myself). He always knew that I would be able to go through the storm to get to the other side, It was only because of His strength that I made it through. I only want His will and His plan for my life.

I say to you now, as you're reading this book, believe that you are healed. His Word says that by the stripes that He took for us, we are healed.

Maybe your storm isn't physical; maybe it's emotional or spiritual. Know that whatever your storm in life, the Lord has given words of comfort for the brokenhearted.

You're healed! Speak those words over yourself, as I had to do, and believe them. Because if He did it for me, He will do the same for you. He shows no partiality.

In the bible there were many healed by Jesus. He healed a man with leprosy who came and knelt in front of Him, begging to be healed. He healed Jairus's dying daughter, who was about twelve years old.

He heals through physicians and medicine. Chemotherapy wasn't pleasant, but I spoke God's Word over the medicine that I was given, and I believe that the Word heals and that this disease, cancer had to bow down to the Word of God.

Through the Word and commands, you are healed, even while being sick. In His Word, He said to a man, "'Stretch forth thine hand.' And he stretched it out: and his hand was restored whole as the other" (Mark 3:5 KJV).

Be willing and believe. Read His Word, understand it, and receive the power that you're given. You must speak over all situations; believe that the Word is greater than what you're facing. Our Lord is still in the miracle-working business. And He'll turn your mourning into joyful dancing.

Remember: Do everything through prayer, be disciplined, surround yourself with faithful friends, and know that it's all in the Lord's timing.

Through His death on the cross and by His stripes, we are healed. Be wise, read, and do your research, do your due diligence. Understand that you must eat the right foods; we all know what they are: fruits and vegetables. Exercise— you don't have to join a gym unless you want to, but do some form of exercise daily, at least three to four days a week (five is even better).

Go for a walk every day, and always remember to stretch your body before and after to maintain flexibility and prevent injury. Workouts will also help to keep up your energy level.

Treat your body with love and care; it belongs to the creator of all things, and your body is His temple.

One thing I must encourage: Don't eat for taste; eat for nutrition. After beginning chemotherapy treatments, your sensory receptors may change. You have to eat even when you don't want to eat. You must feed the medicine; you don't want to regurgitate the medication that's designed to help destroy the cancer cells.

If your stomach doesn't have food in it when the chemotherapy is administered, it can cause you to become nauseous, and the medicine will come up and out of your system. The chemotherapy is a chemical, but it is fighting against the disease that's attacking your body. The chemotherapy must stay in your system to effectively work.

Have a good attitude. Think positively. Speak life and not death; it's in the power of your tongue. "A merry heart doeth good like a medicine: but a broken spirit drieth the bones" (Proverbs 17:22 KJV).

Get out of bed. Lying in bed will take all of your strength, so move as much as possible. Exercise is the best thing you can do. There are benefits to daily exercise. You may feel weak and not have the energy or desire to move, but speak to your body and over yourself saying: "I am healed and I can do this. I can get through this storm and I will! It's already done!"

You have the victory! "And He said unto me, My grace is sufficient for thee: for my strength is made perfect in weakness" (2 Corinthians 12:9 KJV).

I am grateful that I was able to walk every day. When I completed the chemotherapy treatments, walking helped me feel better physically. The muscles in my legs were strengthen, and walking helped my breathing. Getting back into my daily exercise routine was critical for me. My regimens were truly therapy; physically, mentally, and spiritually.

My oncologist impressed on me the importance for a cancer patient to stay active, to do some form of exercise daily. As I walked throughout my neighborhood, I met others that were also walking to maintain a healthy body. Walking to regain my strength was a goal but I also treasured the opportunity to communicate with my heavenly Father. So as I walked daily this was an opportunity for me to have my talks with God. I became more aware of nature, things that we sometime may take for granted. The trees, the wind on our face, you know, we can feel the wind but we can't see it unless we see it moving the leaves on trees and the grass. I enjoyed observing God's creation while walking and talking with Him. I would just walk and observed His many creations; listening to the birds was always and still is so amazingly beautiful.

Permit me to give you one piece of spiritual fitness for the soul:

Read the word and exercise it daily. It will last an eternity.

Like the wind, I couldn't see Him but I could feel Him as a breeze on my face, His presence always with me.

We are not to take nature (e.g., leaves, trees, and animals) for granted; you may wonder how they can survive. The Lord takes care of them and makes provisions for them. How much more will He provide for and take care of us, He who blew His breath into our nostrils?

I was so grateful for what God brought me through. He gave me another chance, another day to serve Him. Thankful for the time I could spend on walks talking to my Lord about all of my concerns, and those things that I thought were so serious. But I soon learned, it was not about me. More importantly, it was a time to listen to, and to wait on God. We just don't want to wait!

It appears we want to move ahead of God, when our concerns are not addressed quickly enough.

During my recovery, I was thankful for another day. And

I wasn't going to sit idle or stay indoors when I was given the green light to get up and out. I was careful not to overexert myself, so I took it slow, but I kept moving.

I was so grateful to be alive, and I wanted to get on with my life. I felt that the Lord spared my life so I could fulfill His purpose for my life. There was work for me to do, and I wanted to get busy.

We sometimes don't realize how much we want to live until we are faced with the possibility that life as we know it, could be coming to an end. I knew that the Lord had promised me some things and I believed that it wasn't over for me, He is faithful and He keeps His promises. This was only a test that I believed I would pass, and that I would be promoted to the next level. His promises are yes and Amen!

I realize after going through, that I had to take the hit. I had to go through with the test to help others. The test I've taken is my testimony to share with others and to encourage them to stay in the race, run with endurance, never give up on God.

Run the race with the One! He will never leave or forsake you.

I knew I must share with others who have been diagnosed with cancer and who are fearful of the unknown, the side effects of chemotherapy, and radiation also life after cancer.

We all need someone to talk to, someone who may have been through or going through what they are about to go through. Someone to talk and share the fears they may have of the unknown of chemotherapy and radiation. Fear is the enemy and can be overcome. You are an overcomer. God brought me through this storm, cancer. He can do the same for you. "For God hath not given us the spirit of fear; but of power, and of love, and of a sound mind" (2 Timothy 1:7 KJV).

You are reading about someone who has gone through this storm and who today is a living testimony. I am a living testimony! What our Lord and Savior did for me, He can also do for you. He shows no partiality.

Recently, other survivors shared their journey through cancer with me. Their stories encouraged me and helped me to finish this book. You have read their testimonies. Each testimony is a blessing and inspiration, they are encouragers. If you are reading this book and have recently been diagnosed, be encouraged! God has brought us through and He can do the same for you. Maybe you have a love one that you think will be helped and encouraged by our stories. I encourage you to share this book.

It is a race to the finish, and you are not alone. You are running this race with the One. By Faith He will see you through to the finish line. Walk if you must; or Run if you can; just don't lay down and give up. Our Savior hasn't given up on you. He is with you every step of the journey. He loves you!

God is so good. He only wants the very best for His children; sometimes, we have to go through uncomfortable times in our lives, but it is not about us. This journey is all about purpose, learning, growing, and being a servant to

God and others. There is a great reward for helping others and knowing that someone is encouraged to run on, to live another day. Don't give up on God, because He don't give up on us.

The Lord created each of us, and He knows how much we can bear. He knows our strengths and weaknesses. It is in our weakness that His strength will be manifested in us. We can do all things through the Lord which strengthens us.

We are asked to cast our cares on Him; why? Because He cares for us.

Scripture says, "And the Lord shall guide thee continually, and satisfy thy soul in drought, and make fat thy bones: and thou shalt be like a watered garden, and like a spring of water, whose waters fail not" (Isaiah 58:11 KJV).

You are victorious. You are more than a conqueror through the Lord. Run the race with the One! My journey began some time ago, but it's not over.

The beginning of what I thought was a nightmare in October 2008, changed my life and strengthen my relationship with God. In October, I made an appointment to visit Methodist Wellness Center for my annual exam. I was diagnosed with an aggressive breast cancer in my left breast. I was not surprised when this lump was detected because I had previously felt it during a self-examination.

But yet I did not want to believe, what I had felt or what I was hearing the oncologist say; the lab report indicates cancer cells in your body, and it is aggressive, the doctor said. We have to act quickly and schedule surgery to remove the tumor.

A lumpectomy was initially what I was told as the course to take. But after further tests it was determined that because the cancer cells were so close to my skin, that it was safer to have a complete removal of the left breast, a mastectomy. And to have the best results, this was to be followed by chemotherapy and radiation.

I immediately went into prayer about this, seeking my Lord and Savior from this point forward. After seeking God in prayer I felt comfortable and at peace to move forward with the plan for surgery.

The surgeon that I chose was preparing to go on vacation, but he wanted to do the surgery himself, and this meant that we had to move quickly. Surgery would be scheduled within a few days of the diagnosis. I was at peace and I was assured that I would have the best surgeon, oncologist, and caregivers possible. The Lord said, "I love you, I'm with you, and all is well."

It's amazing how quickly one can make life-determining decisions. But I trusted God with this difficult decision. I had already prayed about my situation even when I first felt the lump. It is so important to do a self-examination monthly. Early detection is crucial. Be wise! Other prayer warriors were praying with me and for me, and yes I do have a personal relationship with my Lord.

So the life determining situation was in God's hand, not mine, and whether I came out of this situation on this side or with my Father in heaven, it was a win-win situation. I had already heard from the Lord, who is my ultimate physician.

My answer to the doctors was: "Let's do this!"

Both the oncologist and surgeon were believers and very supportive. The Lord had already assigned to me the best doctors and staff as promised. Our Father is a God of excellence. Glory to His name.

The only thing remaining to do was call a family meeting to tell my children, my dad, and my siblings. This was a task that I did not look forward to completing.

Once again, God stepped in and orchestrated the meeting and took control, as I had prayed and asked of Him. My children are positive minded; they are Christians, they love the Lord. They are believers that He is a healer. I shared the doctors' diagnosis, and they were confident and supportive. My family knew that I would be okay, that the Lord was in control of the entire situation.

And we all knew whatever plan He has is the best plan. My children each took turns at the hospital with me, and they alternated days and times after surgery at home. Maurice, my oldest son, spent the first night at home with me; and he did a great job. Ali, my youngest son, was away from home, but his prayers were empowering and were a blessing to me.

Tamika, my oldest daughter, drove me to the first day of chemotherapy treatment; what a blessing to have my daughter available to take me. Both Tamika and Delinda alternated the weekly trips to chemotherapy and many trips to the pharmacy. They were careful to get me home and to ensure I was stable. I thank the Lord for my children family and friends. We need family and friends, their support is half the battle through trials and tribulations. I am so blessed to have such a caring and loving family.

My father, at age eighty-six during this time, was such a strong tower. When I was diagnosed, he was right there, praying and even helped with the repairs to my fence around my home. We had recently incurred storm damages. My sister, my two brothers, their spouses, friends and neighbors were all praying for me. Praise God for the effectual fervent prayers of the righteous man that avails much.

On the day of my surgery, in a room I refer to as the preparation room, before I was given anesthetic. I had a little talk with my Father in heaven, who brought to my remembrance, the "Garden of Gethsemane" where Jesus went to pray before He was taken and crucified.

I realized that God allowed me to understand what it means to trust Him with all my heart. And to know that at some point in our lives we may have to swallow a bitter cup on this tedious journey. We may even ask if the cup could be taken away from us, or if there is another way around it. However, we must be courageous, trust Him and say "Thy will be done in my life". And know without a doubt that He is in control and there is nothing too hard for God. We must trust Him with our whole heart; I will not lean to my understanding but in all my ways I will acknowledge Him, He promised to direct my path.

I did ask Jesus if it were possible that I could bypass this surgery, the chemotherapy, and the sickness to follow. God knew how much I could endure and He knew that He could trust me to help others who were going through. "His Book" He knew would be written and published. This would help others while going through and would provide hope and encouragement. Running this race, no matter how difficult, you can do it. But you must run it with the only "One" who can bring you through it, Jesus is His name.

If He brings you to it, He will see you through it.

I can honestly say that I do not remember much before the anesthetic and very little immediately after surgery, for several hours. I am thankful that I had my talk with the Lord and had a restful sleep through it all. My family told me that I did not open my eyes until I reached my room. I was transported from the operating room, to recovery and after several hours later to my room where family and friends were waiting. They said they road in the elevator with me, but I did not awaken to say anything. A few moans and groans but not awake.

But when I reached my room, I recall stretching my arms forward and motioning for everyone to gather around me for prayer. I remember doing this but yet it was more of a vision or dream rather than reality. I remember opening my eyes, but not able to clearly see or identify anyone. Everyone were like dark figures or shadows.

But I felt the presence of the Holy Spirit and I was led to pray. I remember that I gave thanks to the Lord and

13

prayed. It was a prayer of thanksgiving, for using me and allowing my family and friends to see His miracle. I am a living testimony!

I will always refer to that moment of prayer as the Holy Spirit very much alive and praying, through me

You may have a testimony to a miracle in your life, where you know that without a doubt God did it! As I know that I am a miracle of His healing power. He healed me of cancer. God did it!

I was hospitalized for two days, and when I went home, I was so grateful for the support of my family. They rearranged their schedules to accommodate me, and my grandchildren were able to be at my bedside to also help. I am so grateful and blessed to have such a caring family. So much love and appreciation their action displayed.

I had such wonderful caregivers by my side at the hospital, the nursing staff was great. There was such a great display of love and affection at the hospital and home. A dear friend of mine would prepare food for me, her famous chicken tetrazzini. She is gone to be with the Lord now, but I will always be grateful and I often think of her with much love.

My medication was administered to me hourly, bandages had to be changed and drainage tubes emptied and measured. There were two drainage tubes in my left lower back because I also had thirteen lymph nodes removed; of which two were malignant. Thankful for the help I received, could not have done this alone.

There was still much to do to ensure that the tubes did not become infected after my discharge from the hospital. My children probably were a bundle of nerves. But all was well, they each did a great job as caregivers and prayer warriors. I am so grateful that I had so many people who were concerned and were praying for me. I was told that I had so many phone calls of concern and well wishes. My children even had to answer all incoming calls from co-workers and friends. They were so busy, not only with my medical and physical needs but also with their own personal lives, and work. It is so important to have family with you while going through.

The Lord is so good! He show me daily how much He loves me and that all is well.

Thank you Lord. My children were efficient and made sure the necessities were done. Life goes on, it is comforting to know that your personals are in good hands while you are recovering. Bills still had to be paid.

Trust God. He knows what you need better than you do. He does supply your every need. He assured me that He would provide for me and I would have the best doctors and caregivers. Praise Him! Two weeks passed, and it was time to have the drainage tubes removed from my back; this was my first visit to my surgeon after surgery.

The car ride to the doctors' office wasn't pleasant, the bumpy roads caused a feeling of nausea. Walking from the parking garage into the medical building would seem to be a long walk, and even preparation for the doctor visit was an ordeal when you're in pain. So many small things we take for granted: showering, moving your arms, taking steps from bed to bath. All had become a struggle, but I made it! And so will you!

Oh Lord, I thank you for the activity of my limbs, and for your strength in my weakness.

The removal of the drainage tubes required several visits to the doctors' office. Because there were two tubes, the fluid had to be drained from each tube hourly. The fluid was measured; this was to determine how much fluid was flowing per hour and to determine which tube would be removed first. The tube that drained the least would be removed first, as the second tube was pulling more fluid from my body. My doctor wanted to ensure that all the fluid was drained from the incision area. We did not want a buildup of fluid; this would require another procedure to drain the fluid buildup.

Two weeks later, my second tube was removed, and a week later, I started chemotherapy treatments.

Chemotherapy and radiation, which together lasted eight months. The cancer was considered to be aggressive and had to be treated aggressively. But there is nothing too hard for my Lord.

There were weekly chemotherapy treatments, every Thursday morning, at Methodist Infusion Center. I also received additional chemotherapy, outside of the infusion center of the hospital. This additional dosage was administered while I was at home via the surgical port in my chest. This was a slow drip of chemotherapy that took three days to complete.

I asked my oncologist if I had to have additional chemotherapy, and his answer was yes. Whatever your fear, face it! I always remembered the Lord's Words to me "I love you, I'm with you, and all is well."

Repeating these words kept me calm as I moved forward; I would always remember that I was not going through this alone.

God was with me, and He was greater than any disease, any chemotherapy, or any radiation, and He promised to bring me through this storm.

I believe that the Lord will see you through **it**, whatever **"it"** happens to be. Everything that I'd heard or read about concerning chemotherapy was not pleasant; in fact, it was horrible and frightening. It was not anything that I ever thought I would experience.

I also had radiation treatments; it was explained to me that radiation would be necessary because the cancer was located close to my skin, and the radiation treatments would burn away any residue that wasn't surgically removed.

Chemotherapy began and of course it was nothing I wanted to endure, but I knew I had to go through it. This was my journey that I had to travel to reach my destiny. This is my story to share that it may help others. And for you to understand that what the Lord did for me, He will also do for you. I knew that my journey was greater than I could ever imagine. The Lord know the plans that He has for me and for you. I trust Him even in the midst of the storm that I faced. He is amazing. He is a loving, kind Father. His blessing is rich and adds no sorrow with it.

Although I was going through suffering and sickness, I can say that my faith and peace of mind were intact, and my trust in the Lord was and is rooted and grounded. I realize that He has brought me through and He never left me. Whatever happened as I journeyed through it was all good, a win-win situation. I am still holding on and believing what my Father in heaven told me. He said, "I love you, I'm with you, and all is well."

When you are going through anything, even though you may be suffering or things may look hopeless, you must know that hope is alive and well. Jesus is your hope, and when you have a personal relationship with Him, your hope and trust are in His hands. Nothing is too hard for God. His Word tells us that He is a healer; by the stripes of our Lord, we are healed. We must believe it and receive it today.

As I endured the chemotherapy, the Lord was so good to me: I never experienced nausea, although it is a common side effect. His blessing is abundant and does not add sorrow to it. I did have labs, blood drawn for testing before every chemo treatment; procedure was, if the labs returned normal, the nurse could proceed with administering chemo, but if labs returned abnormal, there would be no administering of chemo that day, you would have to go back home and return the following week with the same process.

But this never my situation, my labs were normal and

I received chemo every week throughout the required treatments.

"How can that be a good thing?" you may ask. Well, because the medicine (chemotherapy) is a chemical used to attack cancer, and for it to attack the cancer cells it must be given and must stay in your system to fight the disease.

Based on lab results, thank You, Lord, I was always able to move forward with treatments. I wanted the medication to fight and destroy the disease. I was never awake through the three hour treatments. I slept until it was time to leave the infusion center. I had additional chemo administered to me by way of a portable intake that took an extra three days. This new chemotherapy was a significant challenge; it made my body feeble. After the completion of the second dosage of chemo, and upon returning to the infusion center, I was given an injection of neulastra to build my immune system.

This injection caused my body to ache and feel feverish. A flu like symptom. These were the most difficult of times. As I think back on those days, I cry, not with sadness but a realization of what God has brought me through. Thank You, Lord. Thank You!

We must trust the Lord when we don't understand what we're facing. Keep your eyes on the prize of the higher calling; don't look to the left or the right but straight ahead. We must look to the author and finisher of our faith. He has given us a comforter (the Holy Spirit) to keep us steady and at peace. This book, my story, spells for me "His-tory," because I have previous experiences with the One!

Can we get through our challenges? Yes, we can! We certainly can.

Chapter 2

Here We Are, Stay Hopeful

In life, you must cope with physical and emotional changes.

I was diagnosed with cancer and went through the process of chemotherapy and radiation.

After treatments, you may find that you are coping with physical distress, and this is expected. But remember to cast your cares for He cares for you.

After the mastectomy of my left breast, I remember getting out of bed and walking to the restroom from my bed.

I stopped and looked at myself in the mirror, particularly the surgical area.

I stood there for a while, gazing at my chest to see if I could notice a difference between my right breast and my left side, where an organ use to be.

I remember thinking of this moment so many times before my surgery and I tried to imagine how I would feel about this day. But at first glance I was amazed at my reaction; which was that of "not much". I really was so grateful to be alive and to be given another chance that it really wasn't a big deal. Only having one breast. It's amazing what becomes important when you are faced with reality. The reality is that I was chosen to go through a battle only to come out with an injury. I still have my life, my family the suffering I endured, I should have lost my mind, But God! He kept me enclosed in my right mind to tell the story of how He brought me through and how He can do the same for others. Honestly. I am truly grateful to be alive, and to even be able to stand in front of a mirror, is only because of His grace. Thankfulness that I survived the surgery and now I can go on with life after cancer. Healed!

My concern was to remove this ugly disease cancer out of my body as soon as possible, even if it meant a mastectomy.

This organ did not define me as a woman or a whole person because of my Lord's assurance to me when He said, "Because of your faith, you are made whole."

I am a woman, a person from the inside out, not only on the outside.

So my first look and thoughts were of gratitude, not anger or bitterness. I chose to be better, not bitter while on my journey of survivorship, I wanted be able to help others get through the process and live life after cancer. And to do this, I had to be healed emotionally, as well as physical healing. I have Hope and I will not give up on God!

The change in your body could produce a positive or an adverse reaction; it's all about how you respond to what you go through in this life, and it determines your overall outcome.

You are given another chance. What will you do with it?

Bitter or better? You make the choice. Choose life, and speak life over yourself. It is in the power of your tongue.

Stay active and always associate yourself with positive people. Stay away from the naysayers.

Yes, you can. Be assured, the Lord has you.

Get busy living or get busy dying.

It's all about how you handle the change that has taken place, but be assured it has not taken over your life unless you give in to it. Move forward; only look back if you must, and only to see how far the Lord has brought you, but do not linger in your past, otherwise how can you step into your future if you are holding on to your past. The past is the past, and the future is filled with hope and the plan that He has for you. Trust God's plan.

Also remember that the choices are endless; you can have reconstruction surgery to replace the organ, or you may decide not to. Give this some serious thought. But be in prayer, and be content with whatever your choice. If your decision is to wait, that's okay; do not be anxious about anything, but in every situation, by prayer and petition, with thanksgiving, present your requests to God.

My surgeon suggested that I wait, and his reasons were valid.

I had drainage tubes in my back; the mastectomy of my breast created open wounds that needed time to heal. My surgeon strongly suggested that I wait, to prevent chances of infection. Reconstruction surgery involves implants; this may cause an infection that could slow down the healing process.

There are other options, such as wearing a prosthesis until you decide. You can be fitted for the correct size, and it can be tailored for you. No one ever has to know.

I write this book in hopes that it will help you with some of your challenging decisions.

I have experienced many of the emotional feelings that you are encountering, and I am hopeful that I can share information that is helpful to you and that you may pass it on to others; Pay it forward.

You may also be dealing with hair loss; if you have chemotherapy, you may experience hair loss.

You may experience weight loss, this is what worked for me: To prevent a drastic weight loss, I would eat even when I was not hungry. But be careful not to overeat because your energy level is very low, and you cannot exercise to lose the excess weight you may gain.

My taste buds were absent; they were not normal as I knew them to be. Nothing had a taste and therefore this discouraged my eating.

Should this also be true for you, the best advice I can offer try to find food that you enjoy. For me, it was chicken and spaghetti seasoned with salt to my taste; it was delicious because I could finally taste.

A very dear friend of mine prepared this meal for me every week because she knew that this was the only food I enjoyed and was able to taste; anything else was like eating air biscuits.

The food digested well, and I was able to regain energy and became more mobile.

My suggestion to you is, when you are feeling a little stronger, take short walks daily, slowly building stamina to increase to longer walks.

You may find that you have little or no energy, not even for a short walk around your home.

What really helped me was B-12 liquid; not capsules or caplets but B-12 liquid which reaches the blood much faster than pills or capsules.

After a few daily doses of the B-12 liquid, you may start to notice an increase of energy.

The daily walk also helps to build muscle and regaining strength in your body.

Remember to drink lots of water; slowly get back into daily workouts, light stretches, and maybe yoga.

Walk and talk with the Lord; ask Him for strength to carry you through this storm.

Began to thank Him as if it is already done; because really it is. Believe it and receive it.

Ask the Lord what would He like you to gain from this storm; is there something He wants you to do?

Is it to help others get through what He has brought you through?

Talk to Him; maybe it has been awhile, and He misses you and wants you to talk to Him more.

He wants a personal relationship with you, always. He is your creator and sustainer. He is your provider and healer.

He is everything that you need, and He supplies your every need.

The Lord, your healer, did not cause your sickness, but He can help you get through it; He helped me. And what He did for me, He will do for you. He has healed me, and He will heal you. Receive it.

By His stripes, which He took on the cross for our sins, we are healed.

Proverbs 3:5–6 says, "Trust in the Lord with all your heart; and lean not unto your understanding. In all your ways acknowledge Him and He shall direct your paths."

"For I know the thoughts that I think toward you, saith the Lord, thoughts of peace, and not of evil, to give you an expected end" (Jeremiah 29:11 KJV).

A Hope and a Future

Remember: it is not over until He says that it is over.

He knows the plan He has for your life; no one can pronounce the end but Him. The Lord knows the end before the beginning.

Do not be distressed or depressed; live your life to the fullest potential, trusting the Lord through it all. Cancer changes you; it is a reality.

But never give up the fight; do not let the change be contrary. Do not let cancer change who you are as a person.

If you fight through it, you will win. It is a done deal. Come to the place where you believe this with all of your heart; trust the Lord with all of your heart and might. He is the 'One' who has sustained you. He is the 'One' who provides for you, the 'One' who healed you, and the 'One' who walks with you. "Run the race with the One".

For if you believe and establish that in your heart and in your spirit, you will have a remarkable and glorious **victory** in the days to come.

"Run the race with the One". **Stay hopeful**.

Chapter 3

Insurance/Assurance

One of my greatest concerns after being diagnosed with cancer was insurance. I had coverage through my employer, but I knew that it was very likely that I would have to apply for short-or long-term disability. Would the insurance cover what could be an extraordinary expense?

I had elected short-and long-term disability coverage with my employer. However, I was still uncertain if the insurance would cover my entire time off from work.

By His grace all things worked together for my good, as He promised in His Word. The short-term disability coverage began after I exhausted my sick leave and vacation time. The Lord is my assurance and is far greater than insurance, and His benefits are out of this world. The rates are affordable. Serving the Lord will pay off after a while.

I contacted my insurance carrier to file a short-term disability claim. They contacted my employer, and the paperwork began. I had given many years of service with the company; they checked for any lapse in insurance coverage and reviewed my work history with the enterprise. There had been no breaks with work, no layoffs due to company downsizing. Just a blessing that I never saw coming.

The insurance company went through a process to determine my eligibility to receive short-term disability and what percentage of my salary I would receive. The representative and the benefits department were very sensitive to my situation and worked to get everything resolved. This was a blessing as it prevented any undue stress for me. They were a blessing in my time of need.

After I was out for several months receiving short-term disability; it was determined that I would need to file for long-term disability, up to twelve months. At this time, I thought the disease required a very long road to recovery.

I kept my focus one day at a time. I knew that I was in good hands and there was no need to worry, no need to fear. The Lord did not give us a spirit of fear, but a spirit of love, power, and a sound mind.

I am grateful that I had peace within, peace that passed all understanding.

I thought about my workplace. Of course, after twenty-one years of service with the corporation, I wanted to remain employed. However, when you're out on disability, you cannot work from home; it would compromise your leave of absence. However, I contacted my manager and offered to call the person who was managing my desk in my absence to assist her in any possible.

But I was informed because I was receiving short-time

and long-term disability, I could not assist with work; it would be a conflict of interest and could jeopardize my benefits. I certainly wanted to get back to my daily work routine and back to what I considered normal. But praises once again to the 'One'. I was never under any pressure to return to work, before time or prior to being released from my doctors.

I reported to my VP in Oslo, Norway; he would contact me at least twice per month. Divine favor from God. The local office manager also contacted me weekly; they both expressed genuine concern and encouraged me to concentrate on recovering and not concern myself with work.

These expressions of interest and genuine concern helped me to stay focused on recovering. I was relaxed and not stressful during my recovery. The genuine concern from management gave me a sense of peace, which also helped in my healing process. Less stress about returning to work enabled me to focus on healing, with peace of mind. Their concern also expressed to me that I was valued as an employee. When you are going through a storm, the support of family, friends, coworkers, and of course prayer is so meaningful and appreciated.

The phone calls and concerns were a blessing and also helped in the healing process; they kept my mind free to focus on me and my recovery. Because of the calls of received, I was no longer focused on trying to get back to the workplace before my body had a chance to heal. Listen to your body. Be sure that you are ready to get back to work physically, mentally, and emotionally because when you return to work, it will be business as usual. You will be expected to get right back to the duties at hand, so it is so important to take the time you need before returning to work.

I would always try avoiding stress because it can slow your healing process. When you are at peace, your mind, body, and soul can rest, you will stay calm and your body will heal.

Emotional and physical healing works hand and hand. When you are free from burdens, knowing that our Lord will never let His children be moved by circumstances and situations, then you can be open to hearing from God.

Psalm 55 says, "Cast your cares on the LORD and he will sustain you; he will never let the righteous be shaken."

Rest is the key ingredient to good health. Ask for wisdom from the Lord; He will grant it to you.

Insurance is a vital asset to have; I am so grateful to have insurance, and I pray for those who do not have coverage. Being diagnosed with cancer can be devastating, but if you do not have insurance, you may feel that you will not get the medical care you need. This alone brings about stress to the mind and the body.

I was contacted by a renowned cancer support group and was asked to speak to a young lady who was preparing to go through chemotherapy; she had been diagnosed with an aggressive cancer and she was afraid. I contacted her, she was from Nigeria but visiting relatives and friends in the United States. She explained she'd been diagnosed with cancer while in her native country but was told that she was in remission. But when she came to the United States, she decided to get another opinion. Her visit to an oncologist here in the US determined that she was not in remission, but had cancer. She needed to have surgery to remove the cancer and would require chemotherapy. She also did not have insurance. She was very concerned, and emotionally upset. Her concerns were receiving quality care without private insurance.

There were so many questions that she asked me concerning my treatments and the type of medication I received. She wanted to compare this with what she was receiving from the hospital that was treating her. She was afraid that she wasn't receiving the best because she did not have insurance. It was revealed later that we were both receiving excellent care; we were both provided the same medication.

My oncologist explained to me that there are several conferences held annually for doctors from all over the world who attend to discuss patient prognosis based on the medication administered. This is discussed to help determine what medications may or may not be destroying the cancer disease. They study what drugs have a positive affect and what can be done to help find a cure, etc.

I encourage all who are reading this book and going through the fight; and I emphasize "going through" because you are going through. Be assured that the battle is won; you are a survivor!

You will make it through to the other side.

The Lord has no respect of persons; what He did for me, He can do for you.

If you have private insurance, this is a blessing, or maybe you do not have private insurance and you are receiving help with your medical treatments through an assistance plan, what a blessing! Do not allow this to burden you, because we have an ultimate physician: our Lord and Savior, He is our healer and His medicine is the best.

He is your **assurance**. By His stripes, you are healed. Whether you have insurance or not, just know that He is carrying you; it is assured in His Word that He has the best plan ever. His coverage is 100% percent, no deductible required, God is not a God of lack! He is the best!

He wants you to draw near to Him with a sincere heart, in full assurance of faith that He loves you. He's with you, and all is well!

The Lord promises are truth. He is right here with you, right now!

He has promised never to leave us nor forsake us. Praise His Holy name.

I was blessed to have a job that offered me great benefits, praise God! which also included short-and long-term disability. After I had exhausted my accrued sick hours and any vacation time that I had, I was able to request short-term disability.

I was blessed to have support and assistance from the benefits department at work, they connected me with the insurance company and an agent who was professional and assisted me every step of the way.

Through this test, God was with me and He promised me that He would be, He is with us, and all is well.

I had His absolute assurance that all would be taken care of for me. The best!

I realize now that I am on assignment. I have a job to complete, and My Father who art in heaven has my back, He is my rearguard and He is meeting my every need. Glory!

I was contacted by the insurance representative, and we discussed my years with the company. I had been with the same company for more than twenty years. There were many forms that my physicians and I had to complete.

These forms were continuous, I had to complete them weekly and were submitted weekly. This was required to receive my disability checks. Praise God, the funds were on time each week; I had more income while on leave of absence than I did when I worked forty hours a week. Nobody but the Lord!

All my needs were supplied, and every bill was paid; I have so much thankfulness to God in my heart and on my lips. It's only because of His goodness that I am here to tell of such goodness.

It may seem crazy to some that I say that; God brought me through all of this so that I can tell of His goodness and

His blessed assurance. But it is true, I would not have made it through without God.

My representatives at the insurance company were so helpful, and I knew that the Lord had his hand over everything. After several months the short-term disability ended, but there was no lapsed time before the long-term disability began (in other words, no break in finances). In all my years with this company, I never filed a disability claim, but with every annual benefit enrollment, I always selected to keep short-and long-term disability benefits as part of my package. And it truly was a blessing to have this coverage.

Thank You, Lord! There is nothing that takes You by surprise. You knew that I would need this coverage. I give You all the glory!

The Lord does not put sickness on you, but He will be with you and never leave you as you go through it. He prepares and equips you, and He already knows what you can endure. He's your creator, your sustainer, keeper and so much more! Rest Assured of His love for you.

I had microscopic out-of-pocket costs, and there were many doctor visits. And I had many prescriptions that had to be filled weekly, from December 2008 through July 2009. Every need was met. I was reimbursed for the out of pocket co-pays and prescriptions.

As I look back over my years with this company, my perspective was that whenever the company sent me on an assignment to Norway, I did not have to pay out-of-pocket costs; the company covered all expenses (e.g., flight, hotel expenses, meals, entertainment, even my laundry cost).

I was on assignment to do a job, and they trusted me to get it done. So they took care of those necessities.

What more would my Father in heaven do for me? I was on assignment for Him, appointed and anointed to do what I have been called to do before the foundation of the world. And the Lord knew that He could trust me to get the job done. All of my needs were met.

I made Him a promise when I said, "Send me and I'll go." I must go even when the cup is bitter.

The Lord met my every need, as He promised, and He blessed me in the process. In everything, give thanks because His blessing is precious, and it adds no sorrow with it.

Be assured. God is our assurance, Paid in Full!

Chapter 4

Tedious Journey, but Joy Comes in the Morning

It was a challenge to come home each week from chemotherapy treatment at the I.V. infusion center. Thursday was not a day I looked forward to. I spent three or four hours in the infusion center receiving chemotherapy treatments.

This was an aggressive cancer that attacked my body. My assigned oncologist said this would require aggressive treatments. This part of the journey was like no other. It was a bitter cup, as I cried out; Lord not my will but Thy will be done.

My chemo treatments were administered at Methodist Hospital in the medical center Houston, Texas. All of the chemotherapy treatments were at this location, every Thursday morning. One Thursday, as I was leaving the hospital, I thought about previous visits to this same building. This is where I came for my annual mammograms.

After checking in for my appointment the nurse would call my name, and I would go in for my mammogram. Every year, I would hear, "You may leave now, Ms. Richardson. Your results are fine." And I would dress and leave, thinking, *Thank you, Lord, that's over until next year.* But October 2008, was a month and year like no other.

I had no idea that one day, I would be at the same hospital, same floor as previous years but not for my annual mammogram procedure but instead I would be having chemotherapy infusions, fighting for my life.

My thoughts *were Lord, I need You more now than I've ever needed You before.*

This was my first day at the infusion center, for my first chemotherapy treatment and it was a little uneasy for me; I did not really know what to expect, athough I had been given a briefing from my oncologist and from other cancer survivors who experienced the same type of surgery as myself and had also received chemotherapy treatments. So they shared with me their stories, and they tried to paint a picture for me, as best they could but this would be my journey.

I knew that I had to travel this road for myself. I was truly grateful for meeting others through the many support groups, and they were a great help to me. Sharing so much valuable information helped to prepare me for what was unfamiliar territory. Although I had been given all this information, on this first day at the infusion center, I could not remember most of what I had been told anyway. My mind was a blank.

Once I entered the center to begin my treatment, only

questions came to mind, over and over again: Would I get sick to my stomach? Would it hurt? How would the chemicals feel going through my body? Would the nurses know what to do?

I had so many thoughts running through my head. I asked one of the nurses if my doctor would be there to make sure everything was administered properly. All these questions were rushing through my mind.

The nursing staff were angels sent by God, they were professionals, well trained and compassionate. The head nurse and others were Christians. I was grateful to God, it was the best as He had promised.

When I arrived and I got off the elevators at the breast center, I checked in and said that I was there for my first chemotherapy treatment. The receptionist was courteous and tried to help me to be calm. Although this was not just a routine doctor visit, it was definitely not a routine doctor visit for me.

But the staff made me feel comfortable and I knew I was in good hands. God's hands and this was soothing to my spirit. I was encouraged that everyone cared and displayed genuine concern for what I was about to go through. I was pleased with my doctor's professional bedside manner; he had many years of experience in successfully treating this disease. But I knew that God is my healer. But to receive the same warmth from the receptionist was encouraging and important to me, as I was about to face the unknown.

My oldest daughter, Tamika, was with me. After checking

in, we sat in the waiting area until I was called to the infusion department. I was so grateful that she was there with me. Tamika and her sister, Delinda, agreed to alternate driving me to the hospital and staying with me through it all.

I am so blessed to have my children; my sons and daughters were there for me. Thank You, Lord, for my earthly father, siblings, children, relatives, and friends. Their prayers and positive words of encouragement were so needed and appreciated. This would have been the most difficult journey without them.

Praises to You, Lord.

As we took a seat, we noticed another lady waiting to go into the breast infusion center; she wore a cap on her head to cover her baldness from receiving chemotherapy. It was December, and it was cold. She spoke to my daughter and I and she asked if we were there to pick up someone from the infusion center.

I told her that I was a patient and this would be my first treatment. She smiled and said she was there for her final chemo treatment. She had a big smile on her face and began to explain that she was so excited to be ringing the bell today. Of course, I wanted to know what she meant about ringing the bell.

She was eager to explain the tradition behind ringing the bell. She explained that this was an exciting time for the patients taking chemo. All the patients looked forward to this day. As a patient you get to ring the bell at the completion of the chemotherapy treatment for yourself. You made it through! Ringing of the bell was a celebration, a time for rejoicing for patients who completed chemotherapy. It was also an encouragement and hope for those still going through it. To celebrate with a fellow survivor and to anticipate that day for themselves.

In essence, never give up hope. If I made it through the treatments, you can too. These were her words. She was an encouragement and an inspiration to me, and I needed that on my first day and not knowing what to expect. I could hear her excitement as she spoke of her accomplishments and blessed to make it through her storm. She did not give up. This was a blessing to hear. I could not wait until it was my time to ring the bell. I was already beginning to look forward to my final day, so I could ring the bell. I began a shout in my spirit, giving God an advance praise.

There is always hope. Keep hope alive, and living in you. Stir up your faith, no matter the situation, you must keep your eyes on Jesus, who is your hope. Remember, as His children, the battle is not ours. It belongs to the Lord. You do not know the path you will have to take on this journey. Trust God, for He knows the plan He has for you.

The Lord never promised that this journey would be easy, but through Him, we can do all things. We are more than conquerors. God promised to be our strength in our time of weakness. This is what helps me to get through, knowing that I am **not** going through anything alone.

I was faced with the reality that I had been diagnosed with cancer and the choice to have surgery, which would be followed by chemotherapy and radiation. The Lord has given knowledge to the doctors to treat different illnesses, but I know that God is my healer. We must trust Him; be prayerful for the doctors, for our families, and for ourselves. Family members need prayer also as they are watching their love one go through this fight and they are feeling helpless, and don't understand what's really going on. When a love one is diagnosed with cancer, it also happens to the survivor's family.

Chemotherapy is a very potent chemical, but I was confident in God to get through it, knowing that He loves me, He's with me, and all is well. Nothing is greater than God.

I had to go through that I may help others, including you who are reading this book right now. Know that God loves you. He will never leave or forsake you, and He is your strength in times of weakness.

Trust Him to get you through. He knows what you can handle and will not put more on you than you can bear. Choose to go through the storm. You are not alone. Stay calm and know that God is with you..

Keep your eyes on the Lord, and you won't drown.

I was told that I would lose my hair, and I did. I was told my fingernails and toenails would get dark, and they did (this does not happen to everyone). A survivor shared their experience with me to help the prevention of my nails darkening. I was told while having chemo injections to place my fingernails in a bowl of ice water would help with the change in coloration. I did this, and it worked for me. I was also told my complexion would darken, I would lose weight, and my eyes would become very sensitive to sunlight and indoor light. Yes, this was true for me.

There are so many reasons to give up as you experience the unknown and the pain that can be so devastating to say no, I can't do this. But yes, you can. You can do it. You can do all things through Him who strengthens you. The Lord is greater than any disease and any situation you may encounter. He will restore, rebuild, and renew you. Trust Him.

I knew that I must live and not die, that I may declare the works of the Lord. I hide His Word on the tablet of my heart. And I could hear Him say the Words that stayed with me, the words that kept me going through the rain and then the storm.

He said, "I love you, I'm with you, and all is well." Nothing could be more present in my mind now. I must hold onto these words and allow nothing less to enter my thoughts: no negative thoughts, never doubting Him. I would make it through this storm.

God had provided for me and brought me through so many trials in past situations. Some situations that I could not see my way clear, but the Lord did it. And what He did for me before, He was more than able to do again. The One who is able to do exceeding, abundantly above all that we ask or think, according to the power that works in us.

I must trust Him when I can't see the end. I realize that

He knows the plan He has for me, plans for good and not evil, plans for a hope and a future.

I believe the Word, and I stand on it and rely on His promises. His Word does not lie. He's always kept His promises to me, including His promise to be with me and never leave me. He loves us, and all is well, and this time in your life is no different. Hallelujah! Thank You, Lord.

I trust You, Lord, with my life; it is not my own. I belong to you. After all, You created me, and You know me better than doctors, nurses, anyone, even better than I know myself. You are in control of all situations, diseases, illnesses of any kind, and that includes cancer. You can make cancer bow down to You and make death behave.

When we entered the infusion center, I saw other women seated in recliners with flat screen televisions at their chairside. I remembering thinking for a brief moment, *Oh, this center is nice.* Then I realized that no one was watching television as if in a relaxed, pleasant place of enjoyment; they were either waiting to receive chemo infusion or sleeping through the process.

My attention was directed to one patient in particular; as we made eye contact. We looked at each other; but no words were spoken, but her eyes said so much. She looked at my face, my hair, and even my attire. Her expression was that of tiredness and weakness in her eyes. I could see that she was tired and weak.

She was draped from head to her feet with warm blankets and wore a knitted cap on her head. Her smile wasn't very big, but just enough to say hello. She looked to be in some discomfort, or maybe she just wanted the whole thing to all be over. I think she may have concluded that this may be my first day. Her eyes glanced at my head and could see that my head wasn't covered, that I still had hair and maybe to her I had a look of uncertainty. She would be correct in her thinking. I definitely did not know what to expect.

The nursing staff directed me to an empty recliner with a flat screen TV also.

My daughter would later watch TV as I slept. I was given information on what would take place. Lab work was ordered and I would have to wait for results, based on the results determined if I could be administered chemo that day. If there are any abnormalities in my blood, I could not have chemotherapy. I would be sent home to return the following week.

I was grateful each week when my blood was drawn, returned normal and therefore I could proceed with the chemotherapy. I was never sent home without receiving the chemo infusion. I never looked forward to having this potent chemicals to enter my body, but I did not want to go home without a treatment and leave a chance for this dreadful disease to rise up in other areas of my body. The Chemotherapy helped to fight the cancer.

The infusion time at the breast center, which included labs and administering of the chemo, resulted in approximately three to four hours. But after each treatment, I was sent home with an additional dosage. I had a slow drip of chemo via a portable unit that was connected to my surgical port. This chemical was placed in a mesh bag, then placed inside a plastic bag that was attached to my undergarment. This chemical was extremely aggressive to fight the aggressive cancer that had attacked my system.

I was instructed by the doctor that if this bag were ever punctured in any way, I must shut off the valve flow and get to the ER as soon as possible. I should explain to the physicians or nurses in the emergency room that I was a cancer patient. The doctors would know what to do. It was also explained to me that if this chemical ever touched my skin, it could strip the skin away from my bones.

This additional chemo dripped slowly into my system and would finish three days later.

This dosage of chemo caused me to become extremely weak in my body and feeling sick. I could barely walk twenty feet before feeling faint. After the third day, I would return to the breast infusion center to have the empty bag removed, and then I was given an injection of a medication "Neulastra" this drug was administered to help boost my immune system and to keep my red and white blood cells normal.

The medication made me feel achy with flu like symptoms: severe body aches over my entire body. I was extremely weak. Other patients who had taken this injection suggested that I take B-12 liquid. After speaking with nurse, she agreed that B-12 liquid would be the most effective. I located the B-12 liquid and purchased it from Whole Foods.

The B-12 liquid worked quicker to reach my blood than the tablets. After each weekly injection of the Neulastra medication I would take a dose of B-12 liquid and it certainly made a big difference in how my body felt, also it's important to stay hydrated.

After the first twenty-four hours of the B-12 liquid in my system, I was able to move around better, and my energy level was increased. The chemo treatments lasted from January 2009 through the end of May. Approximately two weeks later, I began radiation treatments. I did not know anything about radiation, but was told that is not a chemical, it is similar to having an x-ray or CAT scan and would be equally as quick to complete.

I was not so sure that this was true, but I knew that I wanted to go through with the process. Radiation is usually required after chemotherapy and in some cases before to shrink the cancer cell and to destroy cancer cells that could have been missed by the surgery. And this is also a treatment given to extend survival.

There are some side effects to radiation, my mastectomy surgery was of my left breast, near my heart located in the vicinity. I was concerned that the multiple radiations could cause damage and even heart failure in future years. So of course, I was hoping I would not need radiation, but according to my surgeon it was necessary, because the cancer was very close to my skin. Radiation to would destroy any remains of cancer cells. I had thirty-five rounds of radiation treatments.

Radiation began in June 2009, at the hospital annex offsite facility. The staff were very patient and kind throughout my visits. I had no complaints, nothing but gratitude to everyone on the staff.

My initial visit was a consultation to determine the area of radiation that was required and the number of treatments needed. The left side of my chest was marked with a colorful marker and I was instructed not to wash off the markings because the markings are to define the area requiring radiation each visit.

You may ask, with radiation on the same spot over and over again, wouldn't this eventually burn that area of skin?

The answer is, yes, that's the reason for radiation, to burn away any residue of cancer to that skin area. Radiation treatments are designed to burn away what the surgery did not completely remove. Burn the skin and kill the cell. Of course, this was a concern for me. My question was would my skin blister? Would fluid ooze from my skin? Would my skin have first degree burns?

Oh, but the Lord kept me.

I had no burns, even after thirty-five treatments. The radiologist oncologist was amazed and even interviewed me to ask me what was the remedy used to prevent burns to my skin.

I explained that the nurses and the technicians monitored

my area for any noticeable irritations or burns, and I was careful to follow their instructions.

He asked more questions: "Did you ever have burns? Does the area itch?"

No, was my answer. I followed your instructions and the instructions from the staff.

The key was following instructions closely. Do not wear deodorant to radiation appointments; do not use perfume, powder, or perfumed soap (use Dial soap) for bathing. Keep strictly to what the doctors say.

Also, I followed another suggestion that worked for me, and I truly believe it aided in my healing from inside out and prevented the burns. Each day after leaving radiation, I would go directly home and remove my clothes to allow my body to cool from the radiation.

Clothing holds heat; the body needs air after radiation so that it can cool down and stay dry. Your skin is less likely to become irritated and burn with this process of staying cool.

Another suggestion is do not put lotion or powder on the area where you will receive radiation. Even on the days you don't have radiation, keep this area clear of perfumes and dyes.

This is a tedious journey, but I hope that this step-by-step guideline help you, and that you may also pass this information on to others. Isn't that what it's all about, helping one another?

Fighting cancer takes connections and sharing information. The doctors I'm told hold conferences to share what we as survivors tell them and in turn they discuss the different medicines that are being used versus what was administered years ago. We as survivors must help each other and tell the doctors what has helped us. The doctors can then work together to fight against this disease and win!

We need to all work together to kill cancer so that it kills no more.!

Pass it on.

Chapter 5

Be Filled with Knowledge

When I was first diagnosed with cancer, one of my concerns was which doctor to choose. When I received the call from the radiologist about my abnormal mammogram reading, I was given several oncologists and surgeons to choose from.

I did not know any of the doctors by name, so I immediately went into prayer. Scripture says to acknowledge the Lord in everything we do, and He shall direct our path, so I began to pray: "Lord, please reveal to me which physician to choose. I know you told me that I would have the best doctors and nurses, please lead me to them"

I was provided a list of three oncologists and surgeons; I prayed and then selected one of each.

I discovered later through the hospital staff that the doctors I chose were two of the best in their field. I recall hearing the words "Do not fear. I will send you the best doctors and caregivers." The Lord said, "I love you, I'm with you, and all is well."

I was truly blessed to have the best doctors and nursing

staff; they are truly anointed and appointed as caregivers. Glory belongs to God.

Every Thursday, I was always greeted with love and kindness from an excellent nursing staff; they each had such a caring attitude. There were four nurses on duty during my visits, and they each were very professional and super sweet. I was always made to feel comfortable, my questions if any were answered. The nurses all were compassionate and patient with us. They always had a smile on their faces, were attentive to the patients' needs, and displayed the heart of a servant.

There were warm blankets available, snacks, pleasant conversation, and words of encouragement for each of my appointments. It takes a special someone to be a nurse, to have serenity that never seems to end and smiles that never stop, even when the patients are irritated or even angry at their condition, and the emotional rollercoaster they are on that is sometime displayed, the hurt, and the pain endured.

The special someone, the caregiver with the servant heart is what is needed during the times as the survivor is just trying to survive. It's not always easy from both perspectives.

But yet the nurses on staff seem to understand, and their perseverance was limitless. I found it to be remarkable and commendable. I salute you and Thank you for your service!

Glory to God!

My family agreed that the staff was always courteous

and encouraging to them as well. It takes a special someone to have endless patience, even with family of the survivors.

If the nurses were having a rough day, it was never on their faces or displayed in their attitude. They put forth absolute tireless effort. We are so grateful.

I commend the entire staff of doctors and nurses, through it all the nurses stayed focused and were always in a caregiver mode, administering the medication and keeping it all together professionally. Glory to God!

Additional Medication

Along with the chemotherapy, my doctor prescribed an antinausea drug that was administered intravenously.

Some patients develop a rash as a result of certain medications. Thank God my system did not reject the treatments, or the different drugs I had to take along with the chemotherapy in my system. The medications combined helped to fight this disease without me being sick. There were several drugs given intravenously; one medication was administered to help protect my stomach from the harshness of chemotherapy, and there were others to protect my heart.

My oncologist communicated to me his method of treatments and explained the drugs he would prescribe and their purpose and benefit. I am so grateful that my doctor cared enough to share this information with me because as you are watching various drugs being added, you do wonder what is this drug and what reactions will my body have from it. I was so grateful that I trusted God, and recognized that the doctors He sent my way used wisdom and knowledge.

Physical Changes

I will share the physical changes associated with cancer and treatments, but not to alarm you, but to prepare you. Some of these changes are only temporary.

The following physical changes may occur:
- weight loss
- change in skin coloration (may darken)
- skin rash
- discoloration of fingernails (may darken)
- hair loss (also called alopecia)—this is a side effect of chemotherapy and radiation therapy. Radiation therapy and chemotherapy can cause hair loss by harming the cells that help hair growth. Hair loss may also occur throughout the body, including eyebrows, underarms, legs, and pubic area.

I experienced hair loss approximately two to three weeks into chemotherapy treatments and an increase of hair loss one to two months into treatments. Hair loss for me was temporary; it started to grow back a few weeks after I completed chemotherapy and radiation treatments. In most cases, hair will grow back. Full hair growth returned for me within ten to twelve months.

Remember: You can always embrace your bald head;

I received many compliments from family and from total strangers. Or you may decide to purchase a wig (support groups offer wigs, caps, and scarves).

Informational Tips

These are tips for after you start to lose your hair:

- Keep your scalp clean; use a mild shampoo.
- Use sunscreen on your scalp even when you wear a scarf, wig, or cap.
- Avoid chemicals after your new hair grows in (e.g., no perms or hair coloring).
- Allow time for your new growth to grow out, and keep it free of chemicals.
- Don't worry about weight gain or loss. If you lose a few pounds, it's okay; you can gain it back.
- Try not to gain weight because you may not be able to exercise to lose it right away, due to a lack of energy. Overweight is not healthy, monitor your sugar intake, less is better. More water, no sodas.

Physical Changes

Mastectomy: Wearing a prosthetic organ is always an option until you are ready for reconstruction surgery.

Fatigue

Loss of energy can cause you to slow or even discontinue activities that you once enjoyed. This is a temporary factor;

you can eventually regain your strength and build up to your normal routine.

Find a new normal: take walks or exercise in the comfort of your home.

Work out or walk it out with a friend or someone who has gone through similar experiences. Start a walking group; be a support to one another.

Mental and Emotional Changes

In addition to physical changes, you may also have mental and emotional changes.

Dealing with cancer every day is not always easy. Cancer can disrupt a lot of things you considered routine in your life; things are now different. Your usual is now unusual, but you must come to terms with the change and fight against it. No weapon formed against you will prosper. It may form, but it will **not** prosper. Greater is He that is in you than he that is in the world.

Fight the good fight of faith and live! Life and death is in the power of your tongue. Speak **life!** You may feel some anger, some sadness, and some frustration, but you can get through this. Prayer is key and prayer always strengthens you. Have a little talk with Jesus, and after having a talk with the One, everything will start to look a lot better.

Our creator is creator of all flesh and there is nothing too hard for God.

Find the strength in the Lord; He'll show you strength that you didn't know existed.

Peace: His peace passes all understanding. Gratitude is a new attitude. Be grateful to be alive.

Life is unique; enjoy it and cherish every moment. Don't live life being **bitter** but live it getting **better**. Each day is a new mercy and full of the Lord's grace. And His grace is sufficient; it will bring you through anything.

Be thankful. He's our source, He's our provider, and He's our healer. The Lord is in full control. He knows the plan that He has for your life; it's for good not evil, for a hope and a future, and He wants to prosper you.

Life after cancer is the new normal for me, and it can be for you.

Take your time in processing the diagnosis, but the prognosis belongs to my Lord and Savior. Stay calm. Embrace humor. Laughter is good for you and has positive effects on your mind and your body. Be loving, patient, kind, and compassionate. Involve yourself with support groups; those in the group that have been in similar situations. Iron sharpens Iron.

Talk things through with people who have been in the same situation; they can share information and encourage you. And always do a self-talk: "Yes I can! I have the strength to get through this, and on the other side is my victory." I already have the Victory!

In all things, we are more than conquerors through Him who loves us. Stay positive and associate with positive people. Ask for and accept help from the support groups.

Allow others to help with chores around your house,

such as cooking; allow them to prepare meals for you and run errands for you. But also stay as active as possible; this will create energy. Get involved in social activities; this will help redirect your focus.

Give back. Never give up. Pass the baton. Help someone else get through.

You have the victory.

Tell others how you overcame by the words of your testimony. Yes, you can do all things through Him who strengthens you.

Victory is yours.
Be blessed.

Chapter 6

Stay Connected: United We Fight Cancer

The battle is not mine, nor is it yours; it belongs to the Lord.

You must stay focused. There is strength in numbers; let's stay together as survivors, and as believers.

God is a healer, and He will not place more on you than you can bear.

When it seems that you can't make it through another round of chemo or radiation. You can unite together to fight another day. Fight with everything in you, never losing hope.

You are more than conquerors. You are survivors. The Lord challenged me to stand. And when I have done all that I can, I stand. I stand on His promises. His promise is never to leave or forsake me.

He vows to be with you always, even until the end of the earth. I will stand on my belief, on my faith. I walk by faith and not by sight.

The plans and promises the Lord has for me, He will keep. And if you believe His promises, He has a plan for your life too. His plan is for hope and a future, for good and not evil, and to prosper you.

This diagnosis of cancer was a hit that I had to take, so that I could help others who are going through it.

You can get through this. Don't give up, don't succumb to the pain, and don't give in to the sickness. This too shall pass.

Hold on to His Word. He is Jehovah Rafah, our healer. He can do all things but fail. His Word says that He is Lord over all flesh. Is there anything too hard for Him? The answer is no.

> "Come to me, all you who are weary and burdened, and I will give you rest.
>
> Take my yoke upon you and learn from me, for I am gentle and humble in heart, and you will find rest for your souls.
>
> For my yoke is easy and my burden is light." – Matthew 11: 28-30

A setback is just a setup for a greater comeback. When I completed chemotherapy and radiation, my doctor suggested that I take some time for myself. Take time off before returning to work. Time for me to regroup, and think about what I've gone through. Not only physical change but also an emotional battle.

I didn't want to go anywhere, and I especially didn't

want to be alone. But at the same time, I didn't want to go with anyone. I know, it sounds weird, right?

Yes, I know not alone, but also not with others, not with anyone who had not been through what I had gone through and would not truly be able to relate. But I soon had a vision that became an idea that is now a reality. The Lord revealed to me a place that would be a retreat for all cancer survivors and their families. This would be a peaceful place where families could go and spend time together to reflect and to begin the healing process together. I had a vision of a beautiful place with lakes surrounding it and all that nature could offer.

Land and lakes for horseback riding, fishing and so much more. For cancer survivors to be given the opportunity to get their lives back together, living life after cancer.

Joy Comes in the Morning Retreat would offer fishing trips, art classes, access to a library for reading and research, communication with other survivors, counseling with support groups, and much more. We want to educate survivors and families about cancer and the effect it has on the survivor.

JCITMR offers:
- healthy nutrition information and exercise classes
- spiritual and emotional counseling
- Fun weekday and weekend retreats to refresh, renew, and rebuild lives after cancer

- networking with local support groups
- cancer resource information to assist the family in understanding what their loved one has been through

As a cancer survivor, I realize the need for a getaway, to think things over, self-talk, to develop emotional healing, and to spend quality time processing the ravages of a cancer diagnosis. The retreat helps patients become stronger survivors, so they can pay it forward.

Many organizations and research labs are looking for ways to find a cure for cancer; however, survivors need help to rebuild their lives after cancer, one day at a time.

If you are a survivor or know someone who is, and you want to help them receive the resources available through this organization, contact JCIMR (information is listed at the end of this book).

Reach out for yourself or share this book with a loved one.

It doesn't matter if you are recently diagnosed or if you've been a survivor for many years. We still need each other.

Chapter 7

Testing 1, 2, 3. It's Only a Test

If it had not been for You, Lord on my side, leading and guiding me, where I would be?

I could not have made it through without You.

My belief and faith in God has sustained me I am rooted and grounded in His Word. The Word of God is a lamp unto my feet and a light unto my pathway.

If He brings you to it, He will see you through it. His promise is never to leave us nor forsake us.

The Lord is faithful, Somethings we don't always understand, and we ask the question, why Lord and why did this happen to me?

It's not always for us to understand. But if we believe and trust God, He will show us what He want us to learn from what we are enduring. Sometimes, we have to go through some things, our trials come only to make us strong also that we may help others. Some of us really need to know that I can get through this situation; because I see that God brought her or him through and He will do the same for me.

It is a test that we can pass; it may be the same test, or it could be different. But either way, we can pass the test. God is so awesome! He grades us on our test; we are His students, and He's an excellent teacher.

When we pass our test, we are rewarded greatly, and it's always an "A" for absolute obedience.

In the beginning, I did not understand my test. I did not understand why I had to go through what I went through.

But the Lord revealed to me that I was equipped with what I needed to complete the test and pass it.

He equipped me. He prepared me. Preparation is the key.

When you are prepared for battle by the One and Only, you are spiritually, mentally, and physically ready to take on the fight. You can put on the whole armor of faith. But the moment it's time to fight, please take note that the battle is not yours. The Lord will fight it for you. He only wants you to gird up your loins and be ready so that you can endure and persevere through the storm. Peace Be Still! God's in Control.

You will come through the storm, as you trust Him with all of your heart, You live, move, and have your being in Him.

This battle was not one I could ever imagine: as I remember discovering the lump by self-examination. I made an appointment at a medical facility for a well woman visit.

When the doctor examined my breasts, it was determined that there was a lump in my left breast at twelve o'clock position.

I was scheduled for a mammogram and an ultrasound

and was told that I would be contacted within a week with results. I was contacted by phone with results from the ultrasound of abnormalities detected in my left breast.

When I share this part of my testimony, the most common reaction is gasping for breath and disbelief, followed with the question why? I guess if the doctors' visit were more compassionate, maybe my answer when the nurse asked if I wanted to schedule an appointment for a biopsy would not have been no, but thank you.

Of course, I was told the urgency of having the biopsy. The nurse said to me: "Do you understand that this could be serious? You should have the biopsy; this could be cancer."

My answer to her was in the form of a question: "Do you have a cure, if it is cancer?"

The nurse went on to say, "Ms. Richardson, I can't say that we have a cure, but we need to perform the biopsy."

My answer was yes I understand, but I am not going to have the biopsy.

I don't encourage anyone to say no to a test that your doctor may suggest you have done. Although I agree that early detection is important to help fight cancer, But, I believe that I was not ready to go through with the biopsy, at that time and specifically with that doctor. I did not have peace of what may have come after. I know that I needed the right doctors for me, and timing was everything.

I was at peace with my decision; and was not contacted again. But I knew that I was being prepared spiritually for the journey that was ahead of me.

It was the Lord's timing, and then was not the right time or the right doctor. Everything has to line up with His plan. His plans are to prosper us and not harm us, plans to give us hope and a future.

I realize that if I had I gone through unprepared, and out of fear. Without first seeking answers from my Lord, my sustainer and my keeper, whom I go to in prayer this could have been a very different outcome. Right timing, right doctors, only the Best!

The Lord kept me; He held back the growth of the tumor in my breast, He kept it from spreading throughout my body. Thank You, Lord!

The Lord had an assignment for me, He had appointed and anointed me to complete this task. Chosen by God to go through. When you are chosen by the One, have no fear. For He is with you, and He will see you through, Trust and obey His commands and you will not depart this earth before your assignment is complete.

I had to go through some difficult times, a storm, BUT GOD! Stay Calm, it's only a test! Prayerfully my testimony and my perseverance will encourage others to stay in the race. I must let everyone know what the Lord has done for me, and what He will do for you. He has no respect of person, and He shows no partiality.

He has used me, I am His vessel, mouthpiece to tell the story of how I got over! Only by His Grace. He never left me through all that I have gone through. And He will never leave you either. God gets all the Glory! He want others to know that He is everything they need. He is greater than any disease known to man. He can make death behave, anything, anyone must bow down to the mention of His name. There is power in His name. Call on His name, He's waiting.

Be encouraged by my testimony, go through and one day share your testimony; pass it on. Remember, without a test, there is no testimony.

I must let the world know that the Lord can do exceeding, abundantly above all that we ask or think, according to the power that works in us.

I asked the Lord, what was my assignment after going through this, what did He want me to do? I knew that God loved me, He loves me, and that He's awesome and my healer. I knew that what the enemy meant for bad, He had turned all that around for my good. His love is unconditional. He places no conditions on His love; He loves us unconditionally. He is my provider, my protector. He has healed my body, spared my life to live another day; Lord what is my assignment?

There were so many questions, but never was I angry. Instead, I was grateful to be alive, and I knew that I was alive to help others in some way. I am so thankful and grateful that the Lord pulled me through.

I know now that I am assigned to help others that have been diagnosed with cancer and who are going through chemotherapy and radiation. They may be afraid, out of their minds, confused, hurt, and broken hearted. The Lord said help them; you will write it all down and make it plain for others to read and be helped. They will not be able to go through this test alone. They cannot get through the pain, and stress without Me, said the Lord. "You must tell them how you called on Me, and I answered.

So I am telling you, The Lord is your answer, your light through dark times. I want this book to be a guide to what's real, and the reality is the Lord and what He will do for you and how He will bring you through. Man cannot do what He does.

Allow the Holy Spirit to have His way and shine through you as I did in writing His book. This is all about the Lord, His miracles performed, working through me and now you. The Holy Spirit will shine forth, He will direct you, and He will order your steps.

He will awaken a dormant spirit within you. Don't be discouraged; it's only a test.

The Lord has use for you. I must speak the truth and tell my story. I must not fear, only obey His good and perfect will, and do it His way. I believe that God will use me to help millions, and many will be saved. This is not because I am so good, but because He is an awesome God and because I am willing to be used by Him and I will obey because I trust Him with all of my heart,

I must be prepared for volumes; I must go out, go forth, write, speak, and lead lost souls to Him.

Face your test; knowing that you will never face them alone. When you place your trust in God, you are not alone. He will fight your battles; no weapon formed against you shall prosper, and He will never leave you nor forsake you.

His promises are guaranteed; they are, yes! And Amen.

I am also blessed to be the founder and organizer of Joy Comes in the Morning Retreat Ministries. It is a nonprofit retreat ministry envisioned to help cancer survivors and their families become increasingly educated about cancer and treatments available. I am a witness that there is life after cancer.

As you go through any storm in life or test of your faith in God, you are not alone. Also know that the pain and suffering is also felt by your family. Those who are caregivers. I have provided information below if you would like to contact "Joy Comes in the Morning Retreat Ministries". This organization is a blessing and a help for survivors and their families. It provides counseling, support groups networking with other survivors, to provide resources that you may need and so much more.

I give all the glory to my Lord for this book and for "Joy Comes in the Morning Retreat". All glory belongs to Him.

The Lord is so awesome, and I know now that I had to go through this storm. He prepared me, but while on this journey, I have observed families and friends receiving salvation. They were able to experience the miracles performed not only in my life, but also in their own lives.

We see cancer as an awful, dreadful disease, and it is. But just understand that things are not always what they seem. What the enemy means for bad, the Lord turns it around for our good. The devil says cancer, but the Lord calls it a divine appointment to be used by Him. God does not cause sickness; He's a healer and He will go through with you. You already have the VICTORY!!

Will I have to go through another test, another trial?

I don't know if I will, but one thing is sure: I am not alone, and I can do all things through Christ which strengthens me.

We can do it.

Thy will be done Lord.

I will pass the test; I have history with my Father which art in heaven.

He brought me to this appointment, and He saw me through it. If my Father says yes, who am I to say no?

You may say, "Why me, oh Lord?"

I say, "Why not you? Why not me?"

He died on the cross for all of our sins, the sins of this world. It's time that He receive His return on His investment. We should be saying, "Send me, Lord; I'll go."

Resources

Joy Comes in the Morning Retreat

e-mail: info@lourichardsonministries.com

Website: joycomesinthemorningretreat.com

Lou Richardson, founder

Support and certified counseling available

Networking and resources available

1st Book: "Running the Race with the One"

Subtitle: I love you, I am with you and all is well

Author: Lou Richardson

Printed in the United States
By Bookmasters